IMAGES
of America

BOSTON
IMMIGRANTS
1840–1925

In this poignant and evocative photograph, a cooper is shown with the tools of his trade. His strong hand encircles a wood barrel as he gazes off into space. The photograph shows not just an immigrant at work, but the inner determination evident on his face that was shared by immigrants from all countries. As Mary Antin said in her thoughtful book *The Promised Land*, immigrants are the "strands of the cable that binds the Old World to the New." (Courtesy of the Immigrant City Archives.)

IMAGES
of America

BOSTON
IMMIGRANTS
1840–1925

Michael Price and Anthony Mitchell Sammarco

ARCADIA
PUBLISHING

Published by Arcadia Publishing
Charleston, South Carolina

Library of Congress Catalog Card Number: 2008920084

For all general information contact Arcadia Publishing at:
Telephone 843-853-2070
Fax 843-853-0044
E-mail sales@arcadiapublishing.com
For customer service and orders:
Toll-Free 1-888-313-2665

Visit us on the Internet at www.arcadiapublishing.com

Children pose for a photograph at the East Boston Branch of the Boston Public Library on Meridian Street, c. 1915. The first branch library in the United States was opened in East Boston, Massachusetts, in 1871. With the large population surge in this neighborhood after the East Boston Company developed the land in 1833, a wide spectrum of new residents made East Boston their home. The library later instituted an "Americanization Program" that assisted both adults and children in the arduous process of adopting American customs. "The average attendance of children per day during the school year [in East Boston] is between 800 and 900, and there are often as many as 500 in the room at once." Notice the practically empty bookshelves along the wall; these children obviously took reading seriously. (Courtesy of the Boston Public Library.)

CONTENTS

In Lawrence, Massachusetts, the state militia, which included Harvard undergraduates who joined "to help prevent anarchy," forcibly restrains textile mill strikers from marching in the Bread and Roses Strike of January 1912. Members of the militia admitted that they were there to break the strike; one young striking mill worker, a Syrian immigrant by the name of John Rami, was stabbed in the back with a bayonet by a militia member and subsequently died. (Courtesy of the Immigrant City Archives.)

INTRODUCTION

Boston is a city of immigrants, be they descended from the Puritans who settled the Massachusetts Bay Colony in 1630 or immigrants who have recently settled here from Asia, Europe, Africa, or South America. Today, the city is again experiencing an increase in immigration. In the late 19th century, however, immigration had practically ceased after nearly 150 years of steady increase. In the first wave of immigration, between 1830 and 1860, Boston's population increased more than 200 percent, primarily by immigration from Great Britain, Ireland, and Germany. The second wave, between 1860 and 1890, included British, Scandinavians, Germans, Austrians, and northern Europeans. The third wave occurred between 1890 and 1918 and included Slavs, Jews from Poland and Russia, and Italian and Greek immigrants. However, immigration was severely impacted by a 1924 law that restricted new immigrants to those from northern Europe.

Boston is rich in the history of people from all walks of life, from almost every country, and from every ethnicity imaginable. Following the incorporation of Boston as a city in 1822, the city's steadily increasing population and diversity of those seeking refuge from the Old World in the period between 1840 and 1925, created a thriving nexus of cultures that wove together a unique community. The United States, and Boston in particular, has often been referred to as a City of Nations. From the initial settlements in the New World in the 17th century by western Europeans seeking freedom of worship, over the next three centuries, America would attract people from all parts of the world, broadening Boston's ethnicities and religions. By the mid-19th century, Boston's burgeoning population was made up of one-third foreign-born residents.

Often immigrants were rural peasants who were economically depressed. When positive publicity about life in the New World reached them, they set out on a journey that would change their lives forever. Fleeing political unrest and insecurity, often religious persecution and with hopes of a better life elsewhere, many immigrants traveled to the New World in the hopes of making money and eventually returning home. However, in most instances, these immigrants arrived, married, raised families, and remained in their adopted country. With their language, customs, and traditions, these immigrants wove together a community that created a support system within the alien and sometimes hostile New World.

In this book with more than 200 photographs, the authors, Michael Price and Anthony Mitchell Sammarco, have endeavored to create an important and visually stimulating book that chronicles the determination, strength, and often manifold successes of immigrants who arrived in Boston. In chapters dealing with the immigrants before they came to Boston as well as their arrival, their perceptions, and where they worked and played, this book outlines the ancestors of many present-day Bostonians in the evolving process of Americanization.

Mary Antin said in her book *The Promised Land* that upon arrival in America, she and her family gratefully "exchanged *our hateful homemade European costumes*, which pointed us out as 'greenhorns' to the children on the streets for real American machine-made garments, and *issued forth glorified in each others eyes*." (Italics added.) (Courtesy of the Schlesinger Library, Radcliffe Institute, Harvard University.)

One

BEFORE ARRIVAL

Immigrants who arrived in Boston between 1840 and 1925 came from a wide array of countries, often with distinct reasons for leaving their native country. The Canadians in the early 1840s sought employment, and many became shipbuilders and carpenters in East Boston. The Irish began a long immigration in the late 1840s to avoid the famine caused by the failed potato crop. The Swedish sought land, which their native country lacked. The Germans fled the tyranny and social upheavals that led to the Revolution of 1848. The Chinese fled disorder and violence. The Italians and Spanish fled futility, and the Russian and Polish Jews fled oppression and tyranny.

According to the *Boston Herald* in a somewhat patronizing article on April 14, 1896, the immigrants arriving in Boston on the ship *Caphalonia* were composed of

> women wrapped in shawls, bare-headed girls and girls with theatre hats of wirework; brawny, awkward men in high-cut waistcoats and hobnailed boots. They were a strong, clean, healthy-looking set—Irish and English and Scandinavian, with a dozen Italians—642 of them, with ruddy, expectant faces. Most of them were blue-eyed, Celts and Saxons, with well-knit figures and high cheek bones. Several of the girls were quite pretty; their frank, eager countenances and smiling mouths were worth walking a long way to look upon. The men were solid and slow-moving, a hard-headed lot—none of your jaunty, nervous cockneys, but men. And they stood in line, and waited their turn, patiently and well-behaved.

However, less than a decade later in 1903, when the immigrants were more apt to be southern European or Slavic, it was said "the comparatively unrestricted tide of immigration into the United States is in general a menace to the social and industrial life." With an average of 50,000 or more immigrants annually arriving in Boston, it was thought that these hopeful immigrants, who were often illiterate and unskilled, would create a surplus work force and hinder the economy of Massachusetts. The immigrants were stereotyped, often slanderously, in the press with written work and crude political cartoons.

The Emigrant Girl was sketched for the cover page of the February 26, 1859 edition of *O'Neill's Irish Pictorial*. In the two decades before the Civil War, Boston's population was doubled with many thousands of Irish immigrants arriving between 1847 and 1860. They sought a better life from the suffering, hunger, and misery in Ireland that followed the failure of the potato crop in the 1840s, often referred to as "the Great Hunger."

This Irish harvest scene in Kilkenny, Ireland, was sketched in 1852 for *Gleason's Pictorial Drawing Room Companion*. The scene, according to the accompanying newspaper article, represented "a group of laborers in the harvest field partaking of refreshments after the labors of the day. In many districts of Ireland, there are scenes like this which give unmistakable evidence of prosperity, notwithstanding the reports that are constantly reaching us of want and misery in that unfortunate land. It is true that many parts of Ireland have become nearly deserted by reason of the extensive emigration to this country." The magazine was edited by a Yankee and seems ambivalent about portraying the obvious misery that Ireland was experiencing.

Two workers dig in the stone-strewn boglands of Ireland in the late 19th century. The Irish had adversarial relationships with the English and Anglo-Irish landlords and agents who sought to convert overcrowded estates into more profitable grazing lands for cattle and dairy farming. These conversions were facilitated by the land tenure system. The Irish peasant did not own the land, and rents would often be raised, forcing the tenants out should they be unable to pay the rent. Conversion followed the evictions from their cottages.

Hearth and home for the Irish in the 19th century was often a thatch- or potato stalk–roofed cottage with two-foot-thick walls and a hearth stoked with peat to provide both warmth and a place to cook. It was said that an Irish family of six could live for a year on the potatoes that 1.5 acres of land could provide.

Irish peasants pose outside a thatch-roofed cottage in the 19th century. The severe conditions of life in Ireland often led to paupers seeking assistance from the poor relief tax, which was supported by those able to pay often exorbitant rents to landlords. (Courtesy of the John F. Kennedy Library.)

A "famine funeral" proceeds on Old Chapel Lane in Skibbereen, County Cork, Ireland in 1847. Skibbereen was set among rolling green hills with the Ilen River flowing through the town, emptying into the Atlantic Ocean. For all of its picturesque nature, the town was to see massive starvation due to the potato blight. So ravaged was the population that it was said that only the more fortunate of those who died during the height of the famine could afford a coffin. (*Illustrated London News*, February 13, 1847.)

A priest blesses an Irish family, who had survived the famine. They are about to emigrate to the New World, while grieving family and friends gather near their cottage to bid them farewell before their long walk to the port. This heartfelt scene would be repeated many times in the mid-19th century. (*Illustrated London News*, May 10, 1851.)

13

The Irish immigrants arrived at the quay at Cork Harbor, where they saw placards advertising packet passage to Boston, New York, and Quebec. Since the departure for the New World was often protracted; those fleeing the famine were often forced to seek shelter in overcrowded lodging houses before the ships were fully loaded. (*Illustrated London News*, May 10, 1851.)

The *James Baines*, a Train and Company ship, had a tonnage of 2,215 pounds, was 266 feet in length, and operated between Liverpool and Boston. The typical ship would herd 700 immigrants together for 35 days or more to cross the Atlantic Ocean. As an American packet ship, the *James Baines* had a far better reputation for safety and cleanliness than British ships. Train and Company was in direct competition with the Cunard Line, founded by Sir Samuel Cunard.

The Giannelli family poses in Avellino (county), Montefalceone, Italy, c. 1885. From left to right are Concetta, Lucia, Domenic, Giuseppi, Rose, Giuseppi the Elder, and Anthony Gannelli. (Courtesy of Carol Giannelli.)

Mary Antin, the author of the popular book *The Promised Land*, was born in this house, built by her grandfather in Polotzk, Russia. This one-story, wood-framed house with a sleeping attic differed from the Irish cottage since it was an urban, rather than a country dwelling. The Antin house was one of the better-furnished houses in Polotzk, having "upholstered parlors, embroidered linen, silver spoons and candlesticks, goblets of gold, kitchen shelves shining with copper and brass."

Mashke and Fetchke Antin were photographed after their arrival in Boston at the turn of the century. Mary Antin said that "with our despised immigrant clothing we shed also our impossible Hebrew names . . . . The name they gave me was hardly new. My Hebrew name being Maryashe in full, Mashke for short . . . would hold good in English as *Mary*; which was very disappointing, as I longed to possess a strange-sounding American name like the others." Her sister, Fetchke, had her name Americanized to Frieda Antin.

A group of boys studies at a *heder*, or an elementary Hebrew school held at the teacher's residence, in Polotzk in the late 19th century. Note the reverence boys have in reading the scriptures; these boys were referred to as *bahurs*, young unmarried men who were students of the Talmud.

Sabbath loaves, which were wheaten loaves of a peculiar shape and often referred to as *hallah*, are stacked for sale at the bread market in Poltzk. The Russian Jews lived a desperate life, with the ever present threat of pogroms and the desperation of living in the "Pale of Settlement," where Jews were forced to live.

The Jews of the Pale stand around the one kosher meat market in Poltzk.

This photograph shows an Armenian refugee camp in Aleppo, Syria, in the 1920s. These women and young girls had escaped from the devastating conditions in the Armenian sector of the Turkish Empire after the Turkish massacres. Their downtrodden and somber look is both sad and evocative. (Courtesy of Project SAVE.)

Workers transported bananas from the flatland plantations in Jamaica by donkey to the river. The largest banana plantation in Jamaica was owned by the Boston Fruit Company, which had been founded in 1877 by Capt. Jesse Freeman, Capt. Lorenzo Baker, A.W. Preston, and other businessmen who saw the business of exporting fruit to New England grow tremendously by the turn of the century.

Bananas were rafted to the ships that would bring the fruit to Boston. These plantation workers would float thousands of "hands of bananas" during the harvesting season for shipment to New England. With this connection between Jamaica and Boston, many of those who immigrated to New England were already aware of the possibilities of a new life away from their native land.

Enoch Train's White Diamond Line operated between Boston and Liverpool, England, with a weekly sailing bound for America. The ship *Staffordshire* is on an advertising poster showing the list of ships owned by Train and Company and a map showing the distances gauged from Boston. The passengers were described as "young and old, feeble and able-bodied, crowding the pier and the gangway with their luggage, and pouring into the huge, bulky vessel which is to be their home for three or four weeks" before arriving in the New World.

This print illustrates a common practice called "roll call at sea." The ship's officers reviewed the passengers to ascertain the sanitary condition of the immigrants coming aboard the ship. If the immigrants complied with the regulations, the officers reviewed them as they passed up the starboard gangway to the upper deck and returned to the main deck by the port side.

A group of East Indian immigrants, who arrived at Boston c. 1905, poses on the steerage deck of a ship with curious cabin passengers leaning on the railing behind them.

Armenian refugees board a ship for passage to Beirut from Mersine, Syria, *c.* 1920. (Courtesy of the Armenian Library and Museum of America.)

Immigrants from Europe pose on the steerage deck of a ship docking at East Boston at the turn of the century. Notice the difference between the headwear of the women on the right with headscarves and those on the left with straw boaters. A poignant observer noted, "As emigrants, pray tell me who would roam, / When they can stay and starve at home?"

Two

ARRIVAL

Mary Antin describes her excitement upon her family's departure from Russia for the New World: "So at last I was going to America! Really, really going, at last! The boundaries burst. The arch of heaven soared. A million suns shone out for every star. The winds rushed in from outer space, soaring in my ears, 'America! America!'"

East Boston, and Jeffries Point in particular, served as Boston's version of Ellis Island from the 1840s to the early 1920s. Beginning in the 1840s, a large number of Canadians came to East Boston. Donald McKay, a native of Canada, opened his shipyard in East Boston, where he built some of the fastest sailing ships in the world, including the *Flying Cloud*, which set a round-the-Horn record to San Francisco. The Irish soon followed the Canadians. In 1849, it was said that there were about 29,000 immigrants in Boston from all countries, although the majority was Irish. By 1850, there were about 35,000 Irish in Boston, and five years later there were more than 50,000. Many of these new immigrants remained in East Boston, working as low-paid laborers.

By 1885, one-third of Boston's population was foreign born. Following the Canadians and the Irish were Jewish immigrants from eastern Europe and Italians. The initial view of Boston by the immigrants was chillingly described in the book *Out of Ireland*, the memoirs of Tim Cashman, an Irish immigrant:

> [After] some stormy weather, the shores of the new world hove in sight. The port of Boston was our disembarking place, and the wharf on East Boston where we landed was of a miserable forbidding aspect. Dire poverty was to be seen all around, such wretched, horrible tenements with ragged, dirty, hungry looking children playing in the ash-heaps of a nearby railroad.

The thrill of a new life in a New World could quickly fade in the pains of adjustment, but the "bent and heart-sore immigrant forgets exile and homesickness and ridicule and loss and estrangement, when he beholds his sons and daughters moving as Americans among Americans." This assimilation was an important step in becoming an American.

At the beginning of the 20th century, these docks in East Boston were where immigrants to Boston first landed. From here, immigrants spread to other cities, such as Worcester and Lawrence, which were major centers of immigrant employment in the numerous mills. The East Boston waterfront along Boston Harbor had the Cunard Line center with terminals for the Boston and Albany and the New York Central Lines on either side.

Immigrants from Europe catch their first glimpse of America and cheer as the ship enters Boston Harbor. It was said in the April 14, 1896 edition of the *Boston Herald* that the "class of immigrants that comes to Boston is of the best quality for citizenship."

The "Grecian temple" on Rainsford Island in Boston Harbor was an impressive, columned building that served as a hospital for those with infectious or contagious diseases. Built in the 1830s on Rainsford Island (formerly cattle pasture named for its first owner, Edward Raynsford), it was the predecessor of the hospital on Deer Island. In 1895, it became a reformatory for boys.

The View of the New Almshouse on Deer Island in Boston Harbor was etched for *Gleason's Pictorial Drawing Room Companion* in 1852. Designed by Gridley J. Fox Bryant and built of granite in the form of a cross, with four wings radiating at right angles from a center pavilion, the hospital was where immigrants ill with typhus and consumption were to spend their last days of life, poignantly, all within view of Boston—their hoped-for destination. Bryant was a well-known architect who also designed Boston's Old City Hall and the Charles Street Jail.

To Frank Drew Esq

PAT MALLOY,

Originally sung with Immense Success by

his inimitable Character of The Irish Emigrant,

MR. DAN BRYANT,

at Wallack's Theatre

Words by Dion Boucicault Esq

Arranged by John P. Cook Esq

NEW YORK.

Dan Bryant portrayed the character Pat Malloy and sang with immense success "his inimitable character of The Irish Emigrant." Seated on his wooden trunk with rope handles, embossed "Pat Malloy, Parish Kilkenny Ireland," this immigrant stage character of the mid-19th century epitomized thousands of his fellow Irish countrymen seeking a better life in America.

The Deer Island Hospital in Boston Harbor became the place where immigrants ill with typhus, cholera, and other infectious diseases were quarantined after having arrived in Boston Harbor. It was not just the immigrants who died of these illnesses, but often those caring for them. In 1847, Dr. Joseph Moriarity died at Deer Island of typhus; it was said of him that "he had been indefatigable in his attentions to the sick emigrants at the Hospital, and the exposure to which he was subjected probably predisposed his system to the malady which caused his death."

Long Wharf on Boston's waterfront was photographed *c.* 1875, with ships lying at dock. The row of counting houses on the right had direct access to the wharf, which teemed with activity whenever a ship arrived in Boston. (Courtesy of the Boston Athenaeum.)

Looking toward Boston from the East Boston waterfront *c.* 1880, this view shows the tall masts of numerous ships massed along the docks in Boston. The ship *Niagara* was built in 1848, for the Cunard Line and was photographed at the Atlantic Dock in East Boston; the *Niagara* provided crossings from Liverpool, England, to East Boston for cabin passengers and immigrants until sold in 1862. (Courtesy of the Boston Public Library.)

The ship *Istrian* of the Leyland Line lies at dock in East Boston. Photographed in 1876, the East Boston waterfront along Jeffries Point, seen on the left in the distance, was a teeming place of activity. The point also housed the site of the Jeffries Point Yacht Club, the first such club in the United States. Although steam was becoming an accepted means of power for ships by this time, enough people were still leery of it that builders included masts, which, although hardly effective, reassured hesitant passengers. (Courtesy of the Boston Public Library.)

MORE IMMIGRANTS.—Four vessels arrived at this port yesterday, bringing a fresh importation of foreigners, viz : ship Trenton, 171 ; bark Abbot Lord, 176 ; brigs Huron and Woodpoint, 171—making *five hundred and seventeen*. We can find in the English language no terms to express our abhorrence of the rascality of those trans-atlantic moneymakers, who circulate placards about Ireland, whenever there is the least prospect of any work to be done in this country—advising emigrants to set sail for America. Within one week, over *one thousand* Irishmen have arrived in our city, allured hither by these infamous placards, "to build the Long Pond Aqueduct." We have not yet learned how many votes they deposited yesterday, in favor of the project.

This anti-immigrant news item appeared in the May 2, 1845 edition of the *Daily American Eagle*.

A Company of Swedish Immigrants was etched for *Gleason's Pictorial Drawing Room Companion.* These immigrants, according to the editor, were known as "Jenny Lind Swedes, being from the better class of agricultural laborers in their country, and all possessing more or less ample means for forming a permanent and comfortable settlement in this country. They are all Protestant . . . . Seldom does a body of emigrants make so fair an appearance as this delegation of the countrymen of Jenny Lind, the sweet songstress, who greeted us from their fatherland. They were all of them very well dressed, hale and hearty in their appearance, and there were some fifty women in the ranks as they past our office [on the right]." In this view looking down Tremont Street from the Boston Common, these emigrants were considered a better class than most. The article goes on to note smugly, "There is room enough and to spare in our western country for all such emigrants as these. We grieve to see paupers, and such like, arriving from abroad; but when we behold a body of intelligent and well-found emigrants like these, arrived on our shores, we rejoice to extend to them the honest hand of welcome. The party . . . took passage at once by the Western Railroad, via Albany and Buffalo, for the rich agricultural lands to be found westward."

This group of immigrants poses on the steerage deck of a ship at the turn of the century. The enthusiastic boy in the center raises his hand in a salute, possibly returning that of a ship's officer. (Courtesy of the Boston Public Library, Print Department.)

A group of immigrants mills about the dock after having landed at Boston via the *Adriatic* on July 2, 1923. It was said that when the immigrants were allowed to disembark, "down came the joyous people of the steerage on a run, carrying big canvas bags and yellow and black tin boxes and trunks that rattled and banged," all their earthly possessions from the Old World. (Courtesy of the Boston Public Library, Print Department.)

Immigrants arrive on the ship *Carmania* on November 1, 1923, in the race to beat the United States immigration restriction laws of 1924. The large number of immigrants awaiting permission to land in Boston included those from Italy and eastern Europe, whose numbers the new immigration law stemmed. (Courtesy of the Boston Public Library, Print Department.)

The interior of the immigrant processing building in East Boston was a vast space with wooden benches lined up in neat and orderly rows. Inspectors from the immigration department would examine the steerage passengers before they were allowed to enter the United States.

Col. George B. Billings was the immigration commissioner for the Port of Boston at the turn of the century. In April 1896, as the ship *Cephalonia* docked in Boston, "the commissioner of immigration and his six inspectors, accompanied by the reporter of *The Boston Herald*, came ashore and were ready to examine the steerage list in the immigration pen . . . . The inspectors took places at six desks, one at the ends of each aisle, marked off by rope lines." The new immigrants were examined, and those who passed the examination entered into the New World.

A woman and her son walk along a ship's deck after having docked in Boston after a usual voyage across the Atlantic Ocean. The woman balances a rope-tied suitcase on her scarf-covered head as her son carries a small bag of their belongings—their only possessions from their life in the Old World. (Courtesy of the North Bennet Street School.)

These two children sit on a suitcase that is propped up on a steamer trunk at the turn of the century. The girl on the left wears a hat decorated with a ribbon of the ship *Milano*, while her young companion has one of the ship *Andrea Doria*.

A southern German family sits on the wooden benches, awaiting inspection at the Immigrants' House in East Boston, c. 1903.

These Russian Jews await further inspection at the Immigrant House in East Boston. Between 1895 and 1915, there was a dramatic increase in Jews immigrating to the New World from eastern Europe, Tsarist Russia, and Poland.

Immigrants from Finland, then a part of the Russian Empire, await inspection. Finns, or Scandinavians, as they were called, were often described as showing "high quality of character and morals." Of those who immigrated to the New World, only one percent was illiterate, although 93 percent were unskilled.

These three Norwegians were being held for "special inquiry" and were photographed sitting on one of the wooden benches at the Immigrant House. Immigrants were held for special inquiry when their papers were not in order, when they did not pass the medical examination, or when they faced possible deportation to their port of origin.

These immigrants pose at the turn of the century with their only possessions packed in the trunks and suitcases in the foreground. These were their only tangible link with the life they had left in the Old World. It was said in the *Boston Herald* that "the illiterate of all nations represented at their examinations [at Boston] rarely bring up in jail and generally have more stolidity of character" than those literate immigrants who were already naturalized as citizens.

This 1920 photograph of Sabastino and Rosaria Catalono shows members of their family in front of their relatives' grocery store in Lawrence, Massachusetts. The Catalonos had been married in Italy before they immigrated to Boston. This photograph was taken two days after their arrival to send back to the family in Italy as evidence of their safe arrival. Notice the red bananas, a rarity at that time, to the right of the door and the large amount of fresh fruit displayed on either side. (Courtesy of the Immigrant City Archives.)

Three

APPEARANCES
AND PERCEIVED
APPEARANCES

Ralph Waldo Emerson said of the Boston immigrants of the 19th century that the "energy of Irish, Germans, Swedes, Poles, and Cossacks, and all the European tribes . . . will construct [in the United States] a new race, a new religion, a new state, a new literature, which will be as vigorous as the new Europe which came out of the smelting pot of the Dark Ages."

However, the appearance of the majority of immigrants was far different from those already Americanized or from those who had been in America for an extended period of time. The dark, often shapeless clothing of the immigrants was in marked contrast to the ready-made clothing available in the larger cities. However, hard as immigrants might try, they were marked as a "greenhorn" from the moment they passed through customs in East Boston until they consciously, or unconsciously, began to change their appearance and thereby reduce the startling differences so evident in the immigrant classes.

Often, it was not just clothing that marked a person as a recent immigrant, but also their heavily accented English and inability to understand or react to certain situations. Political cartoonists, many of whom were anti-immigrant, expounded upon the differences of immigrants and native-born Americans, often satirizing and demeaning the immigrants in the process. The perceived appearances of most immigrants were a superficial observation. Often one failed to look past the hard and obviously different exterior of an immigrant to find the real person. Perceptions were often blanket judgments; immigrants would be constantly judged until they had become sufficiently Americanized to pass in general society. Most Americans emphasized the public school as an important step to Americanize and assimilate immigrant children. By teaching the children the English language, by preparing them for citizenship, and by incorporating them into American society as quickly as possible, the public schools would, according to one goal of the Americanizers in 1909, "awaken in them a reverence for our democratic institutions and for those things in our national life which we as a people hold to be of abiding worth."

Irish immigrants were often used for cannon fodder and were, in the eyes of many, easily conned. *The Fresh Emigrant* was etched for the cover of the *Yankee Notions* of August 1863. The anti-Irish text read in a brogue, "What an illegant counthry, sure! Faix an' I hadn't put me fut on the ground, a coming off the ship, before a gentleman handed me fifty dollars, an' give me a bran new shute of clothes, wid illegant goold buttons on lem, and towld me he'd take me to Washington, sure and inthroduce me to his Uncle Samuel!" (Courtesy of the Boston Public Library, Print Department.)

This Irishman is shown in straitened circumstances, standing on the quay of Liverpool in this etching entitled *Outward Bound*. He stares at a broadside of Train and Company's packet ship *Daniel Webster* departing for Boston and the hope of good fortune in the New World.

In the etching *Homeward Bound*, the Irishman, having become prosperous in the New World, stands on the quay at Boston and scans another Train and Company broadside that gives the details of the sailing of the packet ship *Cathedral* for the old country. By booking passage home, he could visit family and friends on the "Old Bog" and regale them with stories of his life and material success in the New World.

Thomas Nast, the noted political cartoonist who was virulently anti-Irish, depicted Irish immigrants as subhuman creatures in this cartoon called *The Day We Celebrate—St. Patrick's Day*, which appeared in *Ballou's Pictorial* in 1867. This riot saw a brutal attack on the police by Irish immigrants, who were depicted by the less-than-honest Nast with cornerblocks of "rum" and "blood," two integral ingredients for any riot. (Courtesy of the Boston Public Library, Print Department.)

An immigrant child is held by a hand as he walks along a sidewalk. The children of immigrants, though they spoke their parents' native tongue at home, began the process of Americanization as soon as they started attending schools where English was spoken. (Courtesy of the Boston Public Library, Print Collection.)

An immigrant family crosses the street in either the West End or the North End of Boston, c. 1900. The immigrant areas of Boston were densely settled and, according to Mary Antin, were "where poor immigrants foregather, to live, for the most part, as unkempt, half-washed, toiling, unaspiring foreigners; pitiful in the eyes of social missionaries, the despair of boards of health, the hope of ward politicians."

Mrs. Milaukas poses with her children in a fenced-in yard, c. 1914. (Courtesy of the Immigrant City Archives.)

John and Francis J. Butler were photographed c. 1862. Among the earliest-known photographic portraits of immigrants to East Cambridge, Massachusetts, Butler immigrated to Boston from Ireland c. 1855, settled in East Cambridge, and worked as a laborer. In 1889, Francis, the young son, became pastor of the Church of the Sacred Heart in Cambridge, the largest church in Cambridge during the 19th century. (Courtesy of the Cambridge Historical Commission.)

Agavni "Agnes" Boyajian and Nighohos
Kalashian were photographed in 1910
in Chelsea, Massachusetts. Having
escaped the massacre of Armenians by
the Turks, they settled in Boston. As a
child, Agavni had survived being hacked
by a saber during the 1895 massacre
in Armenia. (Courtesy of Margaret
Kalajian Cummings and Project SAVE.)

An Italian family poses for this c. 1920 portrait in their best clothes. (Courtesy of the Immigrant
City Archives.)

John H. Leighton, second from the right, and his family epitomized the skilled workers; they became involved with the New England Glass Company in East Cambridge, Massachusetts. Induced to emigrate from England, Leighton began work in 1826 as a gaffer, advancing to a master glass manufacturer. Five of his sons followed in their father's footsteps and became glassblowers; another became a machinist in the mold shop of the New England Glass Company, which continued until the 1880s.

Joseph A. Moran Sr. is seated with his grandchildren and pet dog, c. 1905. Moran was a retired glassblower in East Cambridge, Massachusetts. (Courtesy of Virginia Hurley.)

John (Giovanni) B. Frongillo, a dapperly dressed cabinetmaker in Cambridge, poses for this *c.* 1910 photograph. Often, single Italian men lived eight or ten to a room, paying a few cents weekly for rent. (Courtesy of the Cambridge Historical Commission, Charles M. Sullivan Collection.)

The traditional Polish wedding of Katherine and John Serafinowicz was photographed in East Cambridge after their marriage at St. Hedwig's Church in 1913. (Courtesy of Monica Suchecki and the East Cambridge Heritage Center.)

45

The Giannelli family was photographed in Boston's North End in the early 20th century. Shown, from left to right, are the following: (front row) Lucia Giannelli, Anthony Giannelli, and Giuseppi Giannelli; (back row) Dominic, Concetta, and Joseph Giannelli. (Courtesy of the Sammarco family.)

The wedding photograph of Angela Vicari and Peter LoPiccolo was taken following their marriage at St. Leonard's Church in Boston's North End. St Loenard's is the second oldest Italian Roman Catholic Church in the country and has been an important part of the lives of immigrants and their children. (Courtesy of Joseph LoPiccolo.)

A young Chinese merchant sits for his photograph in 1903. Dressed in the traditional clothing of China, this immigrant would seem to retain his foreign views, dress, and speech even as he dealt with business in early-20th-century Boston. "Racial discrimination was so strong against the Chinese, they were forced to form their own small insular circle to help each other and protect themselves," reported the *New England Magazine* in 1903.

Families in Boston's Chinatown were a rarity, especially after the enactment of the Chinese Exclusion Act of 1882, which forbade the general entry of Chinese women to the United States except for the wives of merchants, travelers, teachers, and students. Chinese men who immigrated to Boston often left their parents, sisters, brothers, and wives in China while they toiled in hard circumstances to save money to send home. This family, photographed in 1903, had the father dressed in western clothes, while his family was dressed in traditional Chinese clothing.

The proprietors of a Chinese store were photographed in Boston in 1903. The store provided an opportunity for their fellow Chinese immigrants to socialize, as discrimination and prejudice toward them kept them from wider exposure to work. The *New England Magazine* wrote that a "Chinaman aims to accumulate enough [money] in ten or twenty years to go back and live in comfort the rest of his days on his native soil."

A Chinese Masonic funeral passes down Harrison Avenue, Boston, in the early 20th century to the drone of cymbals and kettledrums as people line the streets to watch the amulet-covered bier pass. A table of delicacies was spread for the departed, which would sustain them in the spirit life. As it was the wish of most Chinese immigrants to have their bones buried in China after their death, the Chinese Consolidated Benevolent Society took responsibility for their return to China; otherwise, they were buried in a lot at Mount Hope Cemetery in Mattapan.

Elizabeth A. Rowling entered the Port of New York with this Bermuda passport of on November 22, 1919, and proceeded to Roxbury, where she was employed in "general work." Her Declaration of Intent, with a "bona fide intention to renounce forever all allegiance and fidelity to any foreign prince, potentate, state, or sovereignty" asked if she was an anarchist, a polygamist, and if her intentions were in good faith to become a citizen of the United States. She became a citizen of the United States on May 20, 1940. (Courtesy of Russell Rowling.)

In 1919, Alice I. Daly came from Monserrat by way of Canada to Boston, where she married George E. Dyett. (Courtesy of Dorothea D. Rowling.)

Cpl. George Dyett served in Company F, 807th Pioneer Infantry in France during World War I. Born in Monserrat, he came to Boston in 1912, where he was naturalized as a citizen of the United States on July 19, 1919. Many immigrants were to become naturalized citizens following military service for the United States in WWI. On the right, Dyett wears a formal suit. (Courtesy of Dorothea D. Rowling.)

A Lithuanian family poses in a cabbage patch in Lawrence, Massachusetts, in 1905. The three young girls in shirtwaist blouses, on the left rear, were mill workers who boarded with the family. (Courtesy of the Immigrant City Archives.)

Four

WHERE THEY WENT

Boston saw tremendous expansion in the 19th century; immigrants from all parts of the Old World adding to the burgeoning population. Most of these new immigrants were uneducated, unskilled rural peasantry. With their arrival, the city was initially hard pressed to assimilate the immigrants into the "Athens of America," as Boston was called in the mid-19th century. To assist in this vital step in the process, Mary Antin wrote,

> The City Fathers provided soap and water for the slums, in the form of excellent schools, kindergartens, and branch libraries. And there they stop: at the curbstone of the people's life. They cleanse and discipline the children's minds, but their bodies they pitch into the gutter. For there are no parks and almost no playgrounds in the Harrison Avenue district . . . and such as there are have been wrenched from the city by public-spirited citizens who have no offices in City Hall.

The housing available to immigrants was just as disheartening. Mary Antin went on to describe her new apartment on Dover (now East Berkeley) Street in Boston's South End, which was typical of most immigrants' new homes in Boston:

> [It consisted of] five small rooms up two flights of stairs with the right of way through the dark corridors. In the "parlor" the dingy paper hangs in rags and the plaster falls off in chunks. One of the bedrooms was absolutely dark and air tight. To us belonged, along with five rooms and the right of way aforesaid, a block of upper space the length of a pulley line across the court and the width of an arc described by a windy Monday's wash in its remotest wanderings.

Immigrants arrived in Boston and often settled with those from the same country, living in such neighborhoods as Boston's North End, the West End, the South End and outside the city proper in South Boston, Dorchester, Roxbury, Charlestown, Brighton, Jamaica Plain, Roslindale, West Roxbury, and Hyde Park. They migrated to other cities and towns in Massachusetts, especially where there was employment in mills and factories, creating a new neighborhood of immigrants who strived to create a sense of community.

By the mid-19th century, Boston was a densely settled city that was changing topographically as well as ethnically. At left, looking from a hot air balloon, one sees the downtown as a densely built up commercial district that would be swept away in the Great Boston Fire of 1872. Once a fashionable residential section known as the South End (not to be confused with the present neighborhood by that name), this area increasingly gave way to commercial encroachment by the early 1860s.

The North End of Boston was the most densely settled area of the city with large numbers of tenement buildings being erected in the late 19th century to provide housing for the ever increasing immigrant population. Below, from the top of the Lincoln Power House chimney, the closely packed, overcrowded buildings of the North End seem to envelop the spire of Christ Church, popularly known as the Old North Church. The church, built in 1723, is the oldest church in Boston.

Established in 1881, the Immigrant House served as a detention center for immigrants who were ill upon arriving in East Boston or whose papers were not in order. Young, single, immigrant women were required by the authorities to remain at the house until claimed by family members or their fiancés. (Courtesy of SPNEA.)

A baby hammock hangs in the yard of an immigrant tenement in Lawrence, Massachusetts, c. 1900. The baby's siblings pose beside the hammock. This photograph is a potent image of the deplorable, unhealthy, and overcrowded conditions in which most immigrants lived at the turn of the century. Tenement apartments were squalid, often filthy places that contained a large cast-iron stove, often unfamiliar to immigrants, and unfurnished rooms. Here, the immigrants reestablished themselves. They "learn[ed] the mysteries of the iron stove, the washboard, and the speaking-tube" and acquired tables, chairs, and necessary beds. With the apartment lighted by kerosene lamps, and heat generated by the stove, these squalid conditions were usually far better than those left behind in the Old World. (Courtesy of the Immigrant City Archives.)

This photograph shows the typical living space of an immigrant family, where cooking, eating, and sleeping took place. The sad and tired-looking mother stands on the right beside the cast-iron stove while her children sit on the bed and a chair. "There were miserable flats of three or four rooms. Or fewer, in which families that did not practice race suicide cooked, washed and ate; slept from two to four in a bed, in windowless bedrooms; quarreled in the gray morning, and made up in the smoky evening; tormented each other, supported each other, saved each other, drove each other out of the house . . . . Beds and cribs took up most of the floor space, disorder packed the interspaces. The center table in the "parlor" was not loaded with books. It held, invariably, a photograph album and an ornamental lamp with a paper shade; and the lamp was usually out of order." It was said in the *New England Magazine* of 1903 that "the most serious tangible menace to the general welfare of the community from the accession of large numbers of immigrants is involved in this tendency to lower the 'American standard of life.' The gradual decline of the standards of employment and of wages in the textile industries" have severely affected the overcrowded and often unsanitary living conditions of the immigrants. (Courtesy of the Boston Public Library, Print Department.)

Fort Hill, once an eminence of 80 feet, was on the present site of Purchase, High, and Oliver Streets. The fashionable residential district with handsome brick row houses faces a park. By the mid-19th century, Fort Hill saw the "increase of business and the erection of warehouses," which led to the wealthy residents moving from the now unfashionable area. Their former houses were swiftly subdivided for the cheap tenements of the new immigrants.

The restaurant of Atwood and Bacon, known since 1826 as the Union Oyster House, is the oldest in Boston. Built by Hopestill Capen, the building at the comer of Union and Marshall Streets in the North End offers an example of an 18th-century building in a densely built up area of the city. During the Revolution, the radical newspaper the *Massachusetts Spy* was printed here by Isaiah Thomas; Louis Phillipe, the future King of France, lived here in exile after the French Revolution.

The Old Baldwin Place Baptist Church was built in 1810 on Baldwin Place off Salem Street in Boston's North End. After its Baptist congregation moved from the neighborhood, the former church was later used by Temple Beth Israel, where Jews worshiped from 1889 to 1920. Today, the Jewish congregation is located in Brookline and is known as Kehillath Israel, a Conservative temple.

Salem Street was a bustling neighborhood with a lively street life—from neighbors talking on a doorstep to street peddlers selling their wares. Irish, Jewish, and Italian immigrants lived in the North End with an admixture of other groups. The spire of Christ Church, popularly known as the Old North Church, is in the right center. This view of Salem Street was taken from Prince Street in 1885.

North Square in the North End was known as the "Italian Quarter" at the turn of the century. The pushcarts in the square are piled high with fresh fruit and produce, and the buildings include the Banca Stabile and Company, the Poto and Company Groceries, the Savonia Restaurant, and the Hotel Italy. At the turn of the century, the North End was inhabited by numerous Italian immigrants who had followed the Irish and the German and Russian Jews, creating, as historian Theodore White in his book *In Search of History* called, an "immigrant ballet [whereby] old stock Protestants gave way to the Irish, who gave way in turn to Italians or Jews." (Courtesy of the Boston Athenaeum.)

Spring Street, which was laid out in 1733 and connected Leverett and Allen Streets, was between Chambers and Poplar Streets in Boston's West End. A densely built up neighborhood of the city, the West End was almost wholly inhabited by immigrants in the late 19th century. Residents shared narrow and crowded sidewalks and had a perennial rubbish heap for a backyard. Boston's West End was later bulldozed as a blighted neighborhood in the early 1960s in an early attempt at urban renewal. (Courtesy of the Boston Public Library, Print Collection.)

Christ Church was built in 1723, on Salem Street, facing Hull Street. This building is one of the oldest places of worship in Boston. It is also where Paul Revere looked for the signal lanterns to warn of the British march on Lexington and Concord. As is shown in this c. 1875 photograph, the neighborhood was comprised of wood-framed houses from the late-18th and early-19th centuries. Though a densely settled area before the Civil War, its population doubled in the late 19th century, primarily housing immigrants.

By the turn of the century, the wood-framed houses had been replaced with brick tenements that greatly increased the housing available for the new immigrants. The row on the left could house dozens of families, whereas the former wooden houses could hold only a few. Through all these changes, the Christ Church remained as evidence of Boston's colonial past in a rapidly changing neighborhood of residents who had no connection to that past.

This 1900 postcard of Salem Street in Boston's North End shows a densely built up street with new brick tenements and numerous shops and food stores lining the old street, catering to the immigrant population. (Courtesy of Joseph LoPiccolo.)

The North End was often referred to as Little Italy by the turn of the century, since a large number of Italian immigrants lived in the neighborhood. In this c. 1900 postcard, men sit along the sidewalk or mill about in the street on a typical afternoon. (Courtesy of Joseph LoPiccolo.)

The Hotel Rome was a large building in North Square (Little Italy) that provided temporary lodging for new immigrants and those visiting family and friends in Boston. (Courtesy of Joseph LoPiccolo.)

Webster Street was a North End alley that had closely built wood-framed houses on either side of a narrow passageway that was legally called a street. Here, children play in the alley at the turn of the century. Webster Street was later obliterated when the Prado was laid out between the Old North Church and Hanover Street in the 1930s. The dense conditions led to health problems. The lack of privacy meant that these alleys were thought evil and squalid, the "evil which must result to the city from allowing so many of its children to grow up in the narrow confines of courts and alleys without ever a day's experience in the . . . country does not need a prophet to predict."

The Paul Revere House was photographed c. 1890 with a sign above the first floor advertising *fabrica sigari Italiani* (handmade Italian cigars). A large square on the center façade sign makes note that Paul Revere lived in this house from 1770 to 1800. Ninety years later, the colonial patriot's former home and silversmith shop was a cigar factory that catered to new immigrants in Boston's North End.

The former Mather-Eliot House was built in 1677 on Hanover Street near Tilerston Street in the North End. Here lived Increase Mather, president of Harvard College, and his son, Cotton Mather. Andrew and John Eliot, father and son ministers of the New North Church, later lived in this house. By 1895, at the time of this photograph, it was known as the Azorean House, a lodging house for Portuguese-speaking immigrants and sailors from the Azores.

61

By the early 20th century, the Paul Revere House, which was built c. 1680 and is the oldest house in colonial Boston, was used as the *Banca Italiana* (the Italian Bank) and the F.A. Goduti and Company Cigar Factory. Neighborhood children and a dapperly dressed, boatered man pose in front of the former silversmith's shop on the first floor that had become a bank providing service to Italian-speaking immigrants a century later. "The Angelo" on the left was a large tenement building with a pressed metal façade. Joseph Everett Chandler restored the historic Revere House in 1907.

Shown is Nashua Street in Boston's West End. The former row houses had been converted to tenement flats to house large numbers of immigrants. Here, clotheslines crisscross the alley separating the buildings with makeshift porches and railings projecting from the rear brick walls. (Courtesy of the Boston Athenaeum.)

A group of friends congregates outside a storefront in Boston's West End at the turn of the century. With no more than 12 feet separating these buildings in some cases, the center of the alleyway sloped toward a drain that emptied into a culvert, such as the one in the left center. Such conditions led to disease and illness.

Union Place, off Wall Street in Boston's West End, was a squalid alleyway that was the home of Mary Antin and her family. With metal fire escapes ascending the side of these mean tenements and no grass or trees, this alley was all most immigrants could either hope for or expect. This condition was a vast improvement, in her eyes, over the life she left in Russia. Antin describes Union Place as a short box of an alley: "two rows of three-story tenements are at its sides, a stingy strip of sky is its lid, a littered pavement is the floor, a narrow mouth its exit."

A group of people sits on the doorstep outside a doorway leading to their tenement flats with shops on either side. On the left is the Jewish Ladies and Gents Restaurant and on the right, J. Deutsch's meat market. Note the cast-iron balustrade running along the second floor, a remnant of the building's once elegant façade.

These children play in an alley that ran between Shawmut Avenue and Washington Street in Boston's South End at the beginning of the 20th century. Noted architect and Irish immigrant Patrick C. Keeley designed the Cathedral of the Holy Cross. The unfinished spire of the church can be seen in the distance; the church was consecrated in 1875.

Wheeler Street was in the Lower End of Boston's South End and had closely built houses that allowed little sunlight to penetrate. Wheeler Street was once described as a "crooked lane connecting a corner saloon on Shawmut Avenue with a block of houses of ill repute on Corning Street." In this view, a young African American boy roller-skates in the center of the street.

Harrison Avenue in the South Bay area of Boston was a place of residence, business, and continuous activity seven days a week. In this view, two women stop to talk on the left as a man looks through merchandise displayed in front of a store on the right. Notice the Boston Elevated Railway in the distance; it connected Dudley Street in Roxbury to Sullivan Square in Charlestown via Washington Street in the South End.

A South End street in the summer months was a never-ending stream of activity from morning until late at night. From children playing in the streets to yelling peddlers or the clop of horse-drawn wagons and carriages, the noise and activity in any immigrant quarter was as loud as it was continuous.

Two children sit on a tenement doorstep in Lawrence, Massachusetts, with a squalid yard strewn with rubbish. In a little bit of doggerel printed in the Lawrence Survey of living and health conditions of that city in 1911, Robert Louis Stevenson is quoted, mocking the ethnocentric view that life is better here than in foreign lands: "Little Indian, Sioux or Crow, / Little frosty Eskimo, / Little Turk or Japanee, / Oh don't you wish that you were me?" (Courtesy of the Immigrant City Archives.)

This banner spans Salem Street in the North End of Boston, with an oval mourning portrait of Pres. William McKinley, who had recently been assassinated, 1901. The early-19th-century wood-framed building on the left, according to noted sociologist Bernie Kramer, has a sign in Hebrew advertising books, scrolls, and shawls. (Courtesy of the American Jewish Historical Society, Waltham, Massachusetts.)

The Great Chelsea Fire of April 12, 1908, destroyed a large section of Chelsea that was home to many immigrants. This view from Klaxine Hill shows the extent of the fire. The fire burned 360 acres of land and destroyed $12 million worth of property before it was finally extinguished. (Courtesy of the Boston Public Library, Print Department.)

A collection and distribution center for food and clothing for those affected by the Great Chelsea Fire was established at the Young Men's Hebrew Association in Boston's West End. The association launched an all out effort to assist those affected by the fire, which had left almost 15,000 homeless, including 5,000 Orthodox Jews. (Courtesy of the Boston Public Library, Print Department.)

Victims of the Great Chelsea Fire line up for clothing and Passover supplies at the Young Men's Hebrew Association in Boston's West End. The generosity of the public and relief organizations to those who lost everything in the fire was heartening. However, many were in shock due to the severity and extent of the fire. Temporary housing was arranged throughout the city. Many victims eventually settled outside of Chelsea, rather than return to their old neighborhoods. (Courtesy of the Boston Public Library, Print Department.)

The bustling activity on T Wharf in Boston in the early morning hours was never more apparent than in this c. 1915 photograph. Fishermen have begun to unload their daily catch from their fishing boats as buyers line up on the right. Through the maze of ropes descending from the ship's masts, the incomplete Custom House tower that was designed by Peabody and Steams can be identified. The tower, considered to be Boston's first "skyscraper," was erected above the center dome of the Greek Revival–style Custom House, which was designed by Ammi Burnham Young and was built on Boston's waterfront in 1847. The scene in the foreground was repeated daily as fishermen offered their catch for the highest bid.

Five

WORK

In *Radicals of the Worst Sort*, the author quotes the daughter of a Russian mender as saying, "If you want a job go to Lawrence [Massachusetts]." This kind of employment information was not limited to New England. One brilliantly colored poster was placed in the center of an Italian village; it showed a family marching to the mill with the father holding a bag of gold. Underneath this image was the saying, "No one goes hungry in Lawrence." These beliefs that work was plentiful and that the head of the family would amass a bag of gold (many immigrants firmly believed that the streets in America were literally paved in gold), brought immigrants to the New World with preconceived ideas of their future lives. The truth was that the jobs available to illiterate, unskilled immigrants were usually menial work in textile mills, the factory, or as day laborers and domestics.

Immigrants often took work that was tiresome, laborious, and usually unwanted by anyone else. With families to feed here or in the Old World, they had a driving and sustained determination to succeed—even with such obstacles as a lack of working skills and a difficulty in speaking English. However, immigrants have always been a resilient group of people, able to work long hours in trying circumstances. They have overcome obstacles to obtain better working conditions and thereby a better life. Work could be classified as handwork, be it stitching, sewing, or tailoring or more difficult jobs, such as shipbuilders, press operators, machinists, mechanics, or ditch diggers.

Shipbuilding in the mid-19th century was often undertaken in East Boston, as the depth of the harbor did not allow for the building of larger clipper ships in other parts of the waterfront. Here, the *Glory of the Seas* is being built in 1869, in the McKay Shipyard on Border Street at the foot of Eagle Hill on White Street. McKay, seen in the top hat to the left of the ramp leading to the ship's hull, built the *Glory of the Seas* on speculation; it was the last clipper ship McKay built.

Donald McKay (1810–1880) was a Canadian immigrant. He was urged by shipping magnate Enoch Train to move his shipyard from Newburyport to East Boston with the plea, "You must come to Boston; we need you, and if you want any financial assistance in establishing a shipyard let me know the amount and you shall have it." After his move to East Boston, McKay began to craft the sleekest and fastest clipper ships afloat. McKay was always considered a thorough gentleman by all that knew him and was equally well respected.

The Atlantic Works in East Boston was located on Border Street near Maverick Square in East Boston. Here, workers inspect machinery that will be installed on ships. The Atlantic Works was the largest manufacturing concern and employer in East Boston for over a century making ships, steel yachts, tugs, and various steam sailing crafts. The battleship US *Sloop-of-War* was built and launched there.

A laborer, probably an Irish immigrant, digs in a culvert under Commonwealth Avenue. Often unskilled upon emigration, Irish men worked as day laborers for a wage. (Courtesy of SPNEA.)

Mill workers at the Pacific Mills Print Works pose on either side of a printing machine in 1914. (Courtesy of the Immigrant City Archives.)

These Irish shoemakers were photographed in Lawrence, Massachusetts, c. 1903 (Courtesy of the Immigrant City Archives.)

Bashara (meaning "Little Jerusalem") was an energetic young Syrian immigrant; he poses here at age 14 with his first sales valise. This photograph—taken in Worcester, Massachusetts, in 1898—and the two following photographs constitute a visual record of Bashara's progress in America from a young Syrian immigrant to a successful American businessman. (Courtesy of Najib Saliba.)

Bashara, on the left, poses with his first horse and team, which he used to peddle dry goods and clothing from door to door. Bashara holds a *houkua*, a smoking device common to emigrants from the Middle East. (Courtesy of Najib Saliba.)

Bashara's store on Grafton Square in Worcester, Massachusetts, was the culmination of many years of hard work and determination. Bashara K. Forzley stands on the right in the American flag–draped doorway of his dry goods store where he sold boy's clothing, hosiery, and underwear, which could be delivered by the company vehicle in the center. (Courtesy of Najib Saliba.)

Women work at long tables in an American flag–bedecked workroom in the Washington Mill mending room in Lawrence, Massachusetts, c. 1900. (Courtesy of the Immigrant City Archives.)

This stunning photograph shows a young textile worker in 1918 standing between two rows of textile weaving looms. The image shows artistry in its placement of the mill worker between the two machines she operated, with the shadow of the bobbins falling across her. (Courtesy of the Immigrant City Archives.)

Louis Prang, an advocate of social democracy, immigrated to America from Germany and established a factory in Roxbury, Massachusetts, where he introduced chromos. Chromos is the act of reproducing oil paintings by a process called chromolithography. Prang used his extensive knowledge of colors to begin his color printing concern; he invented the Prang Method of Art, which was used in the Boston Public Schools for many years.

Prang introduced the Christmas card to the general public in 1875. The lithographs were colorful, attractive cards that not only wished the recipient a Merry Christmas, but utilized appropriate iconography such as reindeer, sleigh bells, and Santa Claus before the advent of mass-produced cards. Small works of art, these colorful cards displayed the "care with which each stone must be prepared, every one adding a color [so that they] are transformed into excellent and artistic imitations of well known oil paintings."

Away, away!
To my love away;
Fly to my darling and greet her to-day;
Tell her I send her a love and devotion,
Wide as the world is, and deep as the ocean.

The Wood Worsted Mill in Lawrence, Massachusetts, was built in 1905. It extended a quarter of a mile along the Merrimac River and encompassed 30 acres of floor space. The factory produced enough cloth at the turn of the 20th century "to belt the earth and festoon the United States from New York to San Francisco." The mill was a major employer; the textile industry in New England was the largest single employer of mill workers. (Courtesy of the Museum of American Textile History.)

A young worker sits at her workbench with an industrial sewing machine, sewing leather heels for shoes, c. 1900.

A young worker polishes the leather uppers of shoes that have just been sewn at the factory, c. 1900. Once polished, the shoes were placed on the rack behind her for delivery to the packing room for shipment to stores.

These women and girls are being taught to sew, by both hand sewing techniques and machine sewing. Although steadily employed, factory girls, as compared with women who went into domestic service, "in the shops never made over six or seven dollars, and them that dressed so well on that, and paid their board, too, made people lift their eyebrows." Those who were in service often perceived it as a step above factory or millwork.

A group of seamstresses poses for a photograph at the turn of the century. It was said that power machine students could train "for greater skill in their work, and instruction that will lead to advancement in the industry and to a better type of American citizenship." Looking back, we cannot be so sure, but hard work and the unions also helped.

The Canney Basket Factory was a small, wood-framed building where baskets of every size were woven for use as produce baskets to coal hods. Here, a group of workers poses in 1881 outside the Lawrence factory with baskets of every size and description. (Courtesy of the Immigrant City Archives.)

A mill manager and workers pose in front of the Indigo dyeing rollers of the Pacific Mills Print Works in Lawrence in 1914. (Courtesy of the Immigrant City Archives.)

The storefront of L. Gottleib, a German grocery store, in Lawrence was photographed with the owner and two clerks in the front, c. 1890. These ethnic stores sold foods known to immigrants and provided a link to their native land with the familiar foods and service in their native language. (Courtesy of the Immigrant City Archives.)

In a storefront, creatively hung with headless chickens and turkeys, are the owner and two clerks of an Irish market in Lawrence, Massachusetts, in 1893. Meats and provisions, as well as fresh turkeys (as the sign advertises) seem secondary to the artistic manner in which these birds have been displayed on the storefront. (Courtesy of the Immigrant City Archives.)

Francis X. Masse was an epicier, providing teas, coffees, and groceries. He is standing on the right in the white coat. In 1881, he emigrated from Riviere Ouelle, Quebec, and opened this store in 1888, at 256 Walden Street in Cambridge. The Masse Hardware Store still occupies this site. Shown, from left to right, are John McAdoo, a teamster; Patrick Curley, a local contractor; and an unidentified man. The young boy seated on the steps is Ernest Masse, the son of the proprietor. (Courtesy of David Masse.)

M. O'Keeffe and Company was a corner grocery store at Dorchester Avenue and Charles Street in Field's Corner, Dorchester. Michael O'Keeffe was an enterprising native of County Clare, Ireland, who in 1895 began a chain of grocery stores that operated throughout the Boston area. So successful was his provision empire that he and two other partners formed the famous chain of First National Stores in 1925. By the mid-20th century, the First National had grocery stores throughout the New England states.

A group of clerks in the O'Keeffe and Company grocery store provided the dedicated service expected by founder Michael O'Keeffe. With bow ties and crisply starched white jackets, these clerks assisted customers with purchases of coffee, tea, sugar, and other assorted goods.

The Haymarket has been a Boston tradition since the 17th century. Here, in front of Quincy Market, a cadre of pushcarts provides a wide selection of fresh fruit and produce in the Dock Square area of the city. The area was infilled in the 1820s, and Quincy Market, designed by Alexander Parris, was opened in 1826, as a provision and meat market. Today, the area is an attractively restored shopping arcade, with the Haymarket still located within walking distance.

A peddler pushes his wagon through Boston's North End in the late 19th century. The houses in the photograph date to the late 18th century. The North End had become a neighborhood of immigrants by this time. (Courtesy of the Boston Public Library, Print Department.)

M. Silverman's redemption center and J. Slotnick's poultry shop were located at 18 Orleans Street in East Boston. Photographed in 1914, men look through redeemable scrap on a tip wagon on the left, while a man watches workmen hang an advertising sign. (Courtesy of the Boston Athenaeum.)

A mustached man peddles a couple around the Lagoon of the Public Garden at the turn of the century. In 1877, Robert Paget introduced the swanboats, today an integral part of Boston's identity, in honor of the opera *Lohengren*. Peddled by sturdy men who were often immigrants, the swanboats offered a pleasant 15-minute ride around the lagoon, but an arduous drive if one was not in proper shape. The townhouses on the left are on Arlington Street; those on the right are on Beacon Street in Boston's Back Bay.

Graichen and Son was a peddling concern that went from one neighborhood to another in Lawrence, Massachusetts, selling wares such as glass, crockery, britanniaware, platedware, brooms, and willow baskets. Oscar Grachien sits in his wagon; he came to America from Germany in 1873. (Courtesy of the Immigrant City Archives.)

Nellie Kiley was the maid of the Bellamy family of Mount Bowdoin in Dorchester, Massachusetts. Often, young Irish girls entered service for a secure position with a respectable family, although they were required to work long hours. Anna M.J. Bellamy (1839–1922), seated at the head of the table, said in an 1879 letter of her Irish maid that "talking all day to no one but Mary, I began to feel I should catch a brogue." On the left is William W. Bellamy; on the right is Arthur M. Bellamy (Courtesy of Robert Bayard Severy.)

Rev. Peter Ronan, pastor of St. Peter's Church in Dorchester, Massachusetts, poses in the church garden in 1898 with seven members of the Sisters of Charity of Halifax, Nova Scotia, who were to staff and teach at the parish school. Daughters of the immigrants often looked to the church as a possible vocation—one that made their parents proud and provided them with a respectable and secure career in serving God, the parish, and their community. (Courtesy of St. Peter's Church.)

Margaret Sutermeister photographed a Gypsy peddler at the turn of the century, posing beside the Sutermeister House on Canton Avenue in Milton, Massachusetts. Gypsy peddlers would offer all sorts of useful merchandise from pipes, tobacco, and brushes for sale, often walking miles from house to house on a daily basis. (Courtesy of the Milton Historical Society.)

A row of storefronts was added at the turn of the century to the front of the once fashionable Harrison Gray Otis House, designed by Charles Bulfinch and built in 1796 at 141 Cambridge Street in Boston's West End. A cobbler shop is on the left; C. Lee Laundry is on the right. Also on the right is the façade of the Old West Church, designed by Asher Benjamin and built in 1806 at the corner of Cambridge and Staniford Streets.

At right, a Chinese laundryman poses in his laundry shop, sporting a straw boater and an umbrella, at the turn of the century. Before the advent of washing machines, laundry work was laborious and illpaid. The Chinese opened numerous laundry shops throughout the city. Notice the string-wrapped brown paper parcels that the laundryman has already done up for customers; the receipts are written in Chinese. (Courtesy of the Milton Historical Society.)

The Griffin brothers, natives of County Cork, Ireland, owned the Lawrence Dairy Farm, which operated in Cambridge, Massachusetts. The farm was in Lexington and they delivered fresh milk throughout the area in this canvas-covered wagon. Here, outside the Griffin House at 2307 Massachusetts Avenue, are John and Pat Griffin. (Courtesy of Julia Griffin.)

A city of Lawrence street-watering cart pauses as the horses drink from a water fountain, c. 1920. These watering carts would spray a fine mist on the dry streets, minimizing dust clouds created by wind or fast carriages or wagons. (Courtesy of the Immigrant City Archives.)

Three Swedish workers are shown through the stone archway of a beehive kiln at the Norton Company. These emery wheels were of a coarse variety of corundum that was used for both grinding and polishing. (Courtesy of the Worcester Historical Museum.)

A smocked Italian woodcarver poses beside a masterpiece of hand-carved mahogany. Often, Italian immigrants were experts at woodcarving, stone carving, and masonry. (Courtesy of the Cambridge Historical Commission.)

Italian immigrant Ralph Trodella, in the center, works at John Reardon and Sons, a rendering plant at 54 Waverly Street in Cambridge. A huge pile of fat is being cut into small chunks, after which it would be rendered (melted down) for soap and tallow. Men clean out the large oak barrels that have seen much use in the rendering plant, c. 1920 (Courtesy of the Cambridge Historical Commission.)

This photograph of young mill workers was taken at the Washington Mills in Lawrence, c. 1906, before child labor laws were enacted. It shows how very young some of the mill work force was at the turn of the century. Sometimes, whole families would be employed together at a mill. (Courtesy of the Immigrant City Archives.)

Newspaper boys pose in 1919 in front of the offices of the Boston Globe with huge stacks of newspapers under their arms. Notice the wire globe directly above the doors, signifying the worldwide news published daily in the *Boston Daily Globe* and the *Sunday Globe*. (Courtesy of the Boston Public Library, Print Department.)

Young boys load mail onto Car 410 at Post Office Square in downtown Boston in 1907. On the left is the Winthrop Building; on the right is the Subtreasury Building and United States Post Office. (Courtesy of Frank Cheney.)

A baker with his young apprentice places dough in a beehive oven with a wooden peel. Many boys often left school when relatively young to work, as they (and more often their parents) saw no point in continuing their education when they could earn a wage and help their families. Working 12-hour days left little time for play. (Courtesy of the North Bennet Street School.)

A group of young girls makes floral bouquets to sell on the streets of Boston, c. 1905.

A young girl makes artificial roses, placing them in holes drilled on a board. Often, these girls, many of whom did not speak English, were underage; the use of child labor was common turn of the century. (Courtesy of the North Bennet Street School.)

Many immigrants worked as day laborers. Here, men lay underground pipes for gas, electric, and telephone service on Massachusetts Avenue at the comer of Commonwealth Avenue in Boston's Back Bay, c. 1910. This procedure, which had cobblestones being stacked on the left along the sidewalk, often stopped streetcars from passing the extensive excavations. (Courtesy of Frank Cheney.)

Laborers dig a trench at Roxbury Crossing, c. 1905. Day laborers would dig ditches, remove paving stones, or lay streets and sidewalks; it was all backbreaking work. The Roxbury Crossing Depot was on the New York, New Haven, and Hartford Line. (Courtesy of Frank Cheney)

Two boys collect discarded wood and pile it onto a small cart for a later sale.

The famous Bread and Roses Strike in Lawrence, Massachusetts, began on January 11, 1912, when Polish women mill workers discovered that their pay was short, due to a new law limiting the hours women were allowed to work (a maximum of 54 hours per week.) Here, the striking mill workers boldly march down the street holding American flags high. (Courtesy of the Immigrant City Archives.)

Striking women mill workers parade through the streets in Lawrence in 1912, waving American flags. (Courtesy of the Immigrant City Archives.)

A photograph of women waving American flags has a crudely cropped photograph of a banner protesting against the IWW, added as a blatant antilabor smear by the local newspaper. (Courtesy the Immigrant City Archives.)

Six

PLAY

Making music in a band, a walk in the woods in Franklin Park, a trip to Revere Beach, a Sunday afternoon picnic with friends from the Old Country—such were the pleasures of the new immigrants. They had little free time and less money, so they relied on simple pleasures of their own making. Often the churches or synagogues played an important part in allowing them to recreate; the sodalities, clubs, and events of the church became a source and an outlet for leisure activity. Church suppers, picnics, and bazaars that raised money for causes that could aid the group as a whole were a source of both recreation and support.

Before films or widespread professional sports, recreation usually meant activities that one created or engaged in directly. Immigrants formed bands through ethnic connections and groups such as the union; they joined marching bands, orchestras, and performing arts groups at the settlement house. Street feasts featured music, constumes, and food, with often an underlying them such as a saint's day.

Food, of course, was a major focus of any time of relaxation or celebration. Familiar food of their birth place was often unavailable here in Boston, except in the homes of family or friends. Food therefore assumed an even greater role in bringing people together and making a simple occasion more festive. Breaking bread in those instances eased the pain of homesickness and the sense of being an outsider; it was central to helping to make a transition from one world to the other.

Members of the Lawrence Motorcycle Club line up their motorcycles along a Lawrence street in this c. 1925 photograph. The club was said to be composed of primarily Irish and Italian mill workers, who obviously enjoyed the thrill of the ride. (Courtesy of the Immigrant City Archives.)

Mill workers, most probably Irish, pose at an outing to Salisbury Beach in the 1890s. Notice how well dressed the workers were, with many of the women wearing fantastic hats. (Courtesy of the Immigrant City Archives.)

This photograph shows a group of Armenian men at a picnic. The man in the center holds a white handkerchief and dances to the music played by his friends sitting behind him. (Courtesy of Project SAVE.)

A group of Lithuanian women enjoys a picnic in Lawrence, Massachusetts, in 1914. (Courtesy of the Immigrant City Archives.)

Armenian men dance at a picnic, *c*. 1915.

Members of the Goldman family pose during a picnic at Franklin Park in Dorchester in the 1920s. The man on the right is Harry Goldman, who was born in Russia in 1882, with the name Yitzok Zvee Mendelovich. When he was coming to the United States in 1900, according to his granddaughter, "another passenger said to him 'You can't go to America with a name like that. You need an American sounding name, like Goldman.' He admired a band leader of the time named Harry Goldman, so he took that name." Goldman, a master tailor, was later a founder of the Women's Industrial Garment Workers Union in Boston. (Courtesy of Jean Goldman.)

Gypsies dance on the Boston Common at the turn of the century. Often referred to as Romanies, Gypsies were thought to have originated in India. With colorful dress and barbaric jewelry, these Gypsie women seem in stark contrast to the men who wear drab colors. Notice the tinker wagons in the distance.

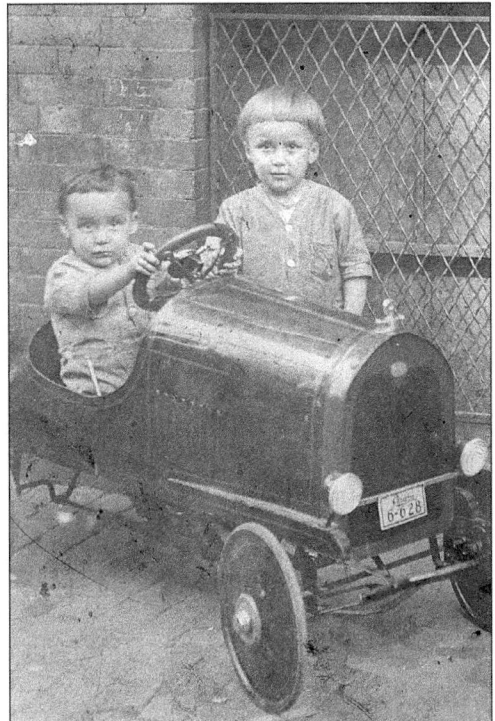

Joseph and David Zanelli pose in front of their home on Minot Street in Boston's West End in 1925 with a photographer's toy car. Photographers would canvas neighborhoods, encouraging parents to have their children photographed with accouterments such as toy cars, ponies, or even horses. (Courtesy of Joseph LoPiccolo.)

Members of a Swedish musical group pose with their instruments and fashionable derbies, *c.* 1905. (Courtesy of the Worcester Historical Museum.)

Members of the Syrian Independent Drum Corps of Lawrence, Massachusetts, pose for a group photograph, *c.* 1919. (Courtesy of the Immigrant City Archives.)

Members of the Bakery and Confectionery Workers International Union (Local 133) in Worcester, Massachusetts, pose with their banner, hand pennants, and caps embossed "Baker's Union," c. 1905. (Courtesy of the Immigrant City Archives.)

The first Lawn Party of St. Peter's Parish on Meetinghouse Hill in Dorchester, Massachusetts, was a swell affair with Irish beauties in white muslin, Rev. Peter Ronan in a Panama hat, and a bountiful collation of hot frankforts. These parties, especially those held by churches, were an important way immigrants socialized. (Courtesy of St. Peter's Parish.)

Children of immigrants are shown in Boston in the early 20th century. The Maypole, with ribbons held by the young girls, signaled the beginning of spring. With younger girls seated around the it, holding bouquets of flowers, and older girls holding ribbons attached to the pole, this scene shows an example of having fun while re-creating an age-old rite. (Courtesy of the North Bennet Street School.)

A group of friends pose on the beach, c. 1905. The dark bathing costumes would be considered immodest in the early 20th century if they did not cover most of the body and include the mop cap to keep one's hair in place. (Courtesy of the Immigrant City Archives.)

The Head House at City Point in South Boston was designed by noted architect Edmund March Wheelwright and was built in 1893. A picturesque example of North Germany half-timbering, the Head House was modeled after a greatly admired building erected by Germany at the Columbian Exhibition in Chicago. With a restaurant on the first floor and bathhouses in the rear, it was a splendid addition to City Point and a popular destination of immigrants, until destroyed by fire in 1942. (Courtesy of Joseph LoPiccolo.)

City Point in South Boston was a popular resort on weekends for all Bostonians in the late 19th century. A convenient place for public bathing, it was serviced by the streetcars; people could get to the beach in minutes from downtown Boston and spend the day there. The South Boston, Puritan Canoe, Mosquito Fleet, and Columbia Yacht Clubs stretched along Columbia Road in the distance. (Courtesy of Joseph LoPiccolo.)

This Italian family relaxes at the beach at Marine Park in South Boston; they seem somewhat overdressed for the beach. The young girl on the right wears a bathing costume of the period, c. 1917. (Courtesy of the Boston Athenaeum.)

In 1909, the city of Boston opened Savin Hill Beach in Dorchester. Here, people walk along the sand as others wade in the waters of Dorchester Bay. The bathing sheds on the left were where one could change into a bathing costume before plunging into the waters off what is today known as Tenean Beach.

The North End Beach was located along Atlantic Avenue. At this time, the Atlantic Ocean was clean enough to swim in. Here, in 1927, North End residents of all ages wade in the cool water, which was a welcome respite from the heat of the overcrowded neighborhood.

Revere Beach was the "people's beach." Hundreds of people traveled from all parts of Boston via the ferry connecting the city to East Boston and then to Revere on the Narrow Gauge Railroad.

The boardwalk at Revere Beach on July 4, 1914, is awash with people who throng the amusements and restaurants during the holiday. On the far right are the amusements and the Ocean Pier, opened in 1911 as a dining and dance hall with a capacity of nearly 4,000 people. There are straw boaters on most of the men; almost every woman wears a hat.

Sitting near the rose pavilion at Revere Beach in 1925 are Rose Giannelli Sammarco, Jennie Giannelli, and Lucia Giannelli. (Courtesy of the Sammarco family.)

Boston's Chinatown, on Harrison Avenue at the corner of Beach Street, is shown in this c. 1905 postcard view. It was only in 1869 that the Chinese Imperial Government relaxed the law that had once made emigration from China punishable by death. After this time, many men left China for the New World and sent money back to support their families, as they never intended to stay permanently. (Courtesy of Joseph LoPiccolo.)

This restaurant in Boston's Chinatown was an elaborately decorated room with silk scrolls, carved woodwork with Chinese motifs, and richly carved, orient-inspired furniture. With such an exotic atmosphere, the brass gasolier in the ceiling seems out of place in its ordinariness.

Chinese merchants take tea in a Boston teahouse in 1903. This room was a clubroom for the merchants to sit and relax during breaks from work, or in the evening, while enjoying a cup of tea. The Chinese immigrants settled together in Boston, creating a miniature version of their homeland that was often referred to as Chinatown by those who viewed it from afar.

An upper room in a Chinese restaurant had an ornately carved table in the center. In the rear of the room is a shrine where the Chinese worshiped and petitioned both the gods and their dead ancestors for such benefits as a prosperous business, continued good heath, and increasing wealth. Often, incense was lighted to please one of the gods or to venerate the spirit of their dead ancestors. On the left and right are rows of armchairs that could be pulled up to the center table.

112

Seven

AMERICANIZATION

Mary Antin described immigration as the "upheaval preceding the state of repose." Without the upheaval in one's life through immigration to the New World, the process of becoming an American could never begin. Americanization has also been described as the trading of one culture for another, which, from today's perspective, might mean losing as well as gaining.

The learning of a new language, customs, and an often very different political system was an arduous challenge, especially for the unskilled male adult whose first priority was employment. Illiteracy was a formidable obstacle to a good-paying job. But how was a day laborer able to find the time for classes? According to the book *Citizenship in Boston*, "the number of persons residing in Boston who cannot read or write the English language is very large and is apt to place Boston in a poor rank among the cities of the country as regards illiteracy." The *Boston American* wrote in 1925, "The State [of Massachusetts] pays one-half the cost and each local community bears the other half." For many immigrants, free education was a new and wondrous experience. Mary Antin writes with amazement and admiration of the American gift of free education:

> Education was free . . . . My father had written about [this] repeatedly as comprising his chief hope for us children, the essence of American opportunity, the treasure no one could touch . . . . On our second day [in Boston a] little girl from across the alley came and offered to conduct us to school . . . we five between us has a few words of English . . . . This child . . . was able to offer us the freedom of the schools of Boston! No application made, no questions asked . . . no fees.

Americanization was an acquired skill, undertaken first by the schools and libraries, which had Americanization classes and later was assisted by the settlement houses. Boston's first settlement houses, which opened in 1891,were Andover House, later the South End House and the Dennison House. By the turn of the century, there were numerous settlement houses in the densely settled neighborhoods of the South End, the West End, and Dorchester. For the immigrant confronted by an often unfriendly citizenry and strange customs, the settlement house was a welcome refuge. These houses taught vocational skills, had health clinics, and provided a place where little girls could "sew, cook, dance and play games; the little boys to hammer and paste, mend chairs, debate, and govern a toy republic." The staff members of the houses, besides providing instruction and moral support, served as valuable role models.

Social workers pose on the steps to the entrance of the South End House. The man on the right foreground is Frank Archey Woods, a noted sociologist who edited *City Wilderness*, a social survey of Boston's South End that was based on practical working knowledge of the poor and immigrant community. Woods served as director of the South End House, which was opened on Rollins Street with various clubs for boys and girls and a literacy society for young adults, all of which were thought important in the Americanization process.

Pauline Agassiz Shaw, daughter of the noted Harvard professor Louis Agassiz, introduced the kindergarten at the North End Industrial Home in 1880. Here, women taught immigrant children the alphabet and other activities at the predecessor to the North Bennet Street School, as it was called after 1885. The North Bennet Street School was "started as a charitable organization to teach immigrant women how to sew and clean so they could find work." The kindergarten and day nursery proved immensely popular, and while "children were playing in the classroom, mothers were free to seek employment," something we are still greatly in need of today more than 100 years later. (Courtesy of the North Bennet Street School.)

Boys wearing shop aprons work in the carpentry class at the North Bennet Street Industrial School at the turn of the century. Sloyd, which was a Swedish version of skilled mechanical work, had been introduced to this country in the late 19th century as a way to work with one's hands, and by so doing learn manual skills and to develop observation skills. Sloyd became part of the school curriculum for domestic science for boys in 1891. (Courtesy of the Boston Public Library.)

A woman looks in the window of a one-room building that was constructed in 1919 in Lawrence by a branch of the YWCA, where unique programs such as English language, sewing, cooking, and canning classes were held for the benefit of neighborhood residents. The YWCA was the parent organization for the International Institute, which assisted the immigrant population in their adjustment to urban America. (Courtesy of the Immigrant City Archives.)

A Celebration of the Holy Ghost of the Portuguese took place in East Cambridge, c. 1907. A young boy wears a crown in the center, with others holding crowns and bouquets of flowers. The American flag is seen on the left and the Portuguese flag on the right—a visual symbol of the past and the present in these Portuguese immigrants' lives. (Courtesy of Kenneth Turino and Chris Mathias.)

A neighborhood clean-up drive in Boston's South End was photographed in 1915. The adage "Cleanliness is next to Godliness" was an important learning tool in trying to make immigrants understand that where they lived had to be kept clean and tidy to deter disease, illness, and germs— something many immigrants were unaware of. (Courtesy of the Schlesinger Library, Radcliffe Institute, Harvard University.)

A group of girls at the Denison House, a local settlement house founded in 1891 on Tyler Street in Boston, learns to weave decorative wicker baskets that were not just attractive additions to their homes, but were the result of a skill that could be expanded upon for a wage after graduation, if they so chose. (Courtesy of the Schlesinger Library, Radcliffe Institute, Harvard University.)

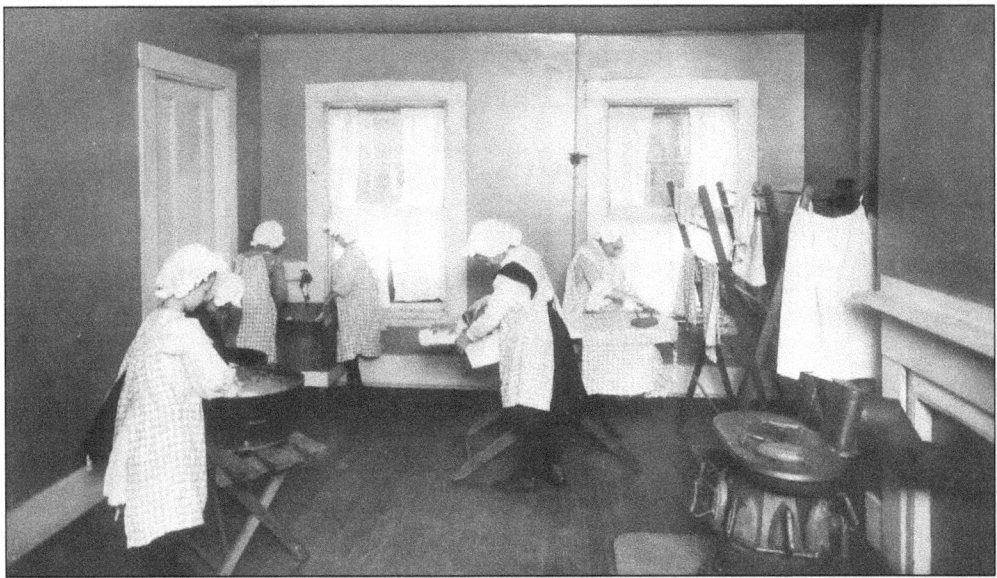

A class of girls in gingham-checked smocks and mop caps washes and irons linens. Learning a skill that would secure a job in the future, these girls might obtain positions as laundresses in the homes of wealthy Boston Brahmins. For most Irish immigrants "in service" was preferable to working in a factory. One such immigrant, Marie Haggarty, said, "If I had gone into a factory to work, the folks would have been worried . . . . I was lots better off. I got seven or eight dollars a week, my room, and it was always a nice one, and the best of food." Others were not as tolerant, one woman saying, "I hate the word service. . . . We came to this country to better ourselves, and it is not bettering yourself to have anybody ordering you around . . . . I tell every girl I know, 'Whatever you do, don't go into service.'" (Courtesy of the Schelesinger Library, Radcliffe Institute, Harvard University.)

The City of Boston's Haymarket Relief Station was located at Haymarket Square between the West End and the North End. Here, medical attention was offered to all Bostonians, especially immigrants, who could often not afford a private doctor and thus become seriously ill without routine examinations. Friend Street flanked the Haymarket Relief Station on the left and North Washington Street on the right; in the foreground is the Haymarket Square kiosk for the subway system.

A "well baby clinic" at the Dennison House encouraged mothers to bring their babies for a routine examination, providing immigrant women with the opportunity of regular medical attention for their children. (Courtesy of the Schlesinger Library, Radcliffe Institute, Harvard University.)

The Dennison House offered plays and other forms of entertainment for the immigrants. The audience was photographed, c. 1915. Although from many different ethnic groups, these entertainments fostered tolerance by joining native and foreign-born citizens in one room. (Courtesy of the Schlesinger Library, Radcliffe Institute, Harvard University.)

The West End Branch of the Boston Public Library was opened in 1896 in the former Old West Church at the corner of Cambridge and Staniford Streets in Boston's West End. This branch library served a densely settled and diversely ethnic neighborhood and had books in foreign languages, books of interest to those in the West End, and programs and exhibits specially geared toward the neighborhood immigrants. (Courtesy of Joseph LoPiccolo.)

These two young women received American flag buttons in the 1912 Independence Day parade in Lawrence, Massachusetts. (Courtesy of the Immigrant City Archives.)

Some 1,200 people attend an evening class for adult immigrants at the High School of Commerce in Worcester, c. 1921, as an orchestra performs on the left. Notice the wide array of foreign flags hanging from the second floor balcony—indicative of the many different immigrant groups attending. These adult evening classes were held to benefit those who worked during the day; trained public school teachers did all teaching. (Courtesy of the Worcester Historical Museum.)

The White Ribbon Society, a Swedish immigrant group, entered this pro-temperance float in the Worcester Midsummer Parade in 1915. The inscription on the float's banner, which reads "For God and Home and Native Land," indicates that these Swedes desired to become good Americans without forsaking their heritage. (Courtesy of the Worcester Historical Museum.)

The National Casket Company of Cambridge, Massachusetts, had a literacy class for its Portuguese and Italian workers to learn English during the lunch break and often for an hour following closing time. These literacy classes were held under the auspices of the YMCA. The two instructors can be seen is in the center with the parts of caskets on all sides. (Courtesy of the Cambridge Historical Commission.)

A class in English was photographed at the Crompton and Knowles Loom Works in Worcester, Massachusetts, in January 1921. Not all workers were so fortunate. A letter of anonymous Polish immigrant (from the *Report of the Commission on the Problem of Immigration in Massachusetts, 1914*) reads, "I am polish man. I want to be american citizen. . . . But my friends are polish people—I must live with them—I work in the shoes-shop with polish people—I stay all the time with them at home, in the shop—anywhere . . . . Better job to get is hard for me, because I do not speak well english and I cannot understand what they say to me. The teacher teach me—but when I come home—I must speak polish and in the shop also. In this way I can live in your country many years . . . and never be good american citizen." (Courtesy of the Worcester Historical Museum.)

Emily Higgs taught English at the North Bennet Street Industrial School in Boston's North End from 1927 to 1937. Despite her threatening demeanor, she was supportive of her immigrant students. Knowing of their difficult lives, she wrote that her students' attendance was irregular due to overtime opportunities at the factories, that they had no time or place to study, and that they were easily distracted. (Courtesy of the North Bennet Street School.)

This English class at the John P. Squires and Company in Cambridge, Massachusetts, met during the lunch break, studying "Lesson Tenth." Squires and Company, one of the largest pork processing factories in the country, had more than 1,000 employees at the turn of the century, many of whom were immigrants who took advantage of this "Noon Class." (Courtesy of the Cambridge YMCA.)

The Quong Kow Chinese School was established in Boston's Chinatown. The mission of the Quong Kow School was to educate first-generation Chinese immigrants and to assist them in learning English. Here, students pose outside the school with a man on the far right holding a drum of Troop 34, Boy Scouts of America, emblazoned with Chinese characters.

A pin party at the International Institute for Young Women in Lawrence, Massachusetts, had a large number of women posing for a group photograph in 1917. (Courtesy of the Immigrant City Archives.)

Boys eagerly await a storyteller in the auditorium in the basement of the East Boston Branch, Boston Public Library in the 1920s. The story hour was sponsored by the library's Americanization Committee, which was established in the early 1920s to familiarize the children of immigrants with the customs and traditions of the United States. "The Americanization Committee has attempted to stimulate the use of libraries by the foreigner, and to that end many special books in simple language on civics and Americanization have been put on the shelves" of the Boston Public Library. (Courtesy of the Boston Public Library.)

A class of girls at the Hyde School in Boston's West End participates in the daily "Sewing Hour." Sewing was a part of the domestic science classes instituted in 1891, by Mary P.T. Hemenway, a dedicated member of the Boston School Committee. It was Hemenway's vision that these girls would be able to sew for themselves, or for a wage, upon graduation. It was said that "sewing reflected a commitment to moral and social advancement." Sewing also enabled these girls to assist their mothers with the necessary mending of the family's clothing. (Sammarco collection.)

Posing in dresses they made themselves are girls at the Wells School in Boston's West End. The Wells School, built in 1868, was expanded in 1914 for the increasing number of children living in the neighborhood. By the mid-19th century, the students in the public grammar schools of Boston had reached 9,850—an increase of 280 percent in 20 years. According to the *Boston Almanac* of 1849, a "small majority, about 50 more than the whole number, *are the children of foreign parents!* This fact alone is of infinite moment; since it shows that the city of Boston is educating a host of aliens *in the principles of our puritan ancestors.*" Mary Antin said that not only was public education free, it was "the essence of American opportunity, the treasure that no thief could touch, not even misfortune or poverty." The public schools were perceived as the chief instrument of Americanization. (Sammarco collection.)

Members of a cooking class at the Bowdoin School prepare food in 1893 on the western slope of Beacon Hill, considered a part of the West End of Boston. In these domestic science classes, which were instituted in 1891, girls learned the proper way to prepare foods, cook them, and serve them. It not only allowed them practical experience that they could use at home, but prepared them for a possible career as a domestic or as a waitress in a restaurant following their graduation. (Sammarco collection.)

Mop-capped and aproned girls work in the "Cookery Class" at the Bowdoin School on Boston's West End in 1893. The Boston School Committee had adopted sloyd, or woodworking for boys, cooking for girls, and a kindergarten system for youngsters in the city's public schools. (Sammarco collection.)

126

A beaming young lady with a star-surmounted headdress holds a cape of red and white stripes with her blue gown festooned with white stars for a one-of-a-kind Independence Day outfit. Her obvious pride in the "Stars and Stripes" made her the perfect example of a proud Americanized immigrant.

Members of the Arlington Mill Marching Band pose for an unique following an Independence Day parade in Lawrence, Massachusetts, in 1923. With distinctive red, white, and blue costumes and the leader in front holding a cloth shield, these mill workers epitomized the Americanization process. (Courtesy of the Immigrant City Archives.)

ACKNOWLEDGMENTS

This photographic book on Boston's immigrants is an outgrowth of an exhibit on the same subject that was held at the International Institute of Boston in 1997. With a major photographic exhibit curated by Michael Price and a lecture entitled "The Boston Immigrant Experience" by Anthony M. Sammarco, its appeal to Bostonians was quite evident in the overwhelming response; this photographic history is the result.

We would like to extend our sincere thanks to the following: the American Jewish Historical Society; Anthony Bognanno; the Boston Athenaeum; the Boston Public Library, Print Department, and Sinclair Hitchings, the keeper of prints; the Cambridge Historical Commission, Charles Sullivan, director; the Cambridge YMCA; Frank Cheney; Margaret Kalajian Cummings; the Giannelli family; Julia Griffin; Virginia Hurley; the Immigrant City Archives; Hannah Gartazoghian Kalajian; the John F. Kennedy Library; Joseph LoPiccolo; David Masse; Chris Mathias; Evelyn Abdalah Menconi; the Milton Historical Society; the North Bennet Street School; Alice Owens; St. Peter's Church, Dorchester, Massachusetts; Project SAVE; Dorothea Rowling; Russell Rowling; Dr. Dennis Ryan; Najib Saliba; Anthony and Mary Mitchell Sammarco; Rosemary Sammarco; the Schlesinger Library, Radcliffe College; Robert Bayard Severy; the Society for the Preservation of New England Antiquities; Monica Suchecki; Amy Sutton, our editor; Robert Bayard Severy; Kenneth Turino; Virginia M. White; and the Worcester Historical Museum. We would especially like to acknowledge the creative work by Barbara Filo, an acclaimed Boston photographer, who traveled and re-photographed many of the original images for the exhibit "The Boston Immigrant Experience," which was held at the International Institute of Boston in 1997, and to Miriam Ovissi, who gave tremendously of herself to make that exhibit possible.

128

www.ingramcontent.com/pod-product-compliance
Lightning Source LLC
Chambersburg PA
CBHW080850100426

42812CB00007B/1982